KARATE
in a week

David Mitchell

Headway · Hodder & Stoughton

ACKNOWLEDGEMENTS

The author and publishers gratefully acknowledge the contributions of Eliza Maeshiro 3rd dan, Taro Shindo 3rd dan, Law Ly Ming 4th kyu and Richard Hurd 4th kyu to the making of this book.

British Library Cataloguing in Publication Data
Mitchell, David
  Karate in a week.
  I. Title
  796.8

ISBN 0 340 56420 2

First published 1992

Typeset by Rowland Phototypesetting Ltd, Bury St Edmunds, Suffolk. Printed in Hong Kong for the educational publishing division of Hodder and Stoughton Ltd, Mill Road, Dunton Green, Sevenoaks, Kent by Colorcraft Ltd.

CONTENTS

INTRODUCTION

WHAT IS KARATE?

Modern karate is a Japanese fighting system that uses high powered punches and kicks to defeat the opponent. It developed on the island of Okinawa, which is roughly midway between China and Japan. Nowadays Okinawa is a part of Japan, but it wasn't always so.

A brief history

The ancient kingdom of Okinawa traded with China and as part of the treaty of 1372 between the two countries, a group of Chinese families was sent to live on Okinawa. Some of the members of these families taught Chinese martial arts to the Okinawans.

The Chinese systems combined with native Okinawan fighting arts to produce **karate**, or 'Hand of Ancient (T'ang) China'.

There were many different forms of karate, and these could be grouped together and named according to the Okinawan city in which they were practised. **Naha te** ('hand of Naha') and **tomari te** were practised in the cities of those names, whilst **shuri te** was practised in Okinawa's ancient capital. Naha te and tomari te later merged to form **shorei ryu**, whilst shuri te became known as **shorin ryu**. Incidentally, the word **ryu** means simply 'tradition'.

Okinawan teachers travelled to mainland Japan during the early part of the twentieth century and set up karate schools there. The best known of these is Gichin Funakoshi, an Okinawan schoolteacher. Funakoshi used to write poetry under the pen-name **Shoto** ('waving pines'), so the school he set up in Japan was called simply 'Shoto's Club', or the **Shotokan**.

Funakoshi developed the shorin ryu training which he had received on Okinawa and eventually the style of karate practised at his training hall also became known as **Shotokan**. This had long, deep stances, powerful movements, and used a lot of muscle power.

Funakoshi was not the only Okinawan to come to Japan and open a club. Chojun Miyagi had trained in Okinawan shorei ryu and the style he developed – **goju ryu** ('Hard/soft tradition') – used short, high stances and circular movements. Kenwa Mabuni had trained in both shorin and shorei schools, so the style he founded is a mixture of the two. It is called **shito ryu**, this being a play on the names of two of his teachers.

Many Japanese students excelled in karate and one of them, Hironori Ohtsuka, left Funakoshi to establish his own Japanese karate school – the **wado ryu** ('Way of Peace Tradition'). This style uses light, fast movements coupled to skilful evasions.

INTRODUCTION

These, then, are the four major styles of classical karate practised today. They are all essentially similar, and it is possible for a student of one style to train with those of another style.

In addition to these, there are other styles such as Masutatsu Oyama's **kyokushinkai** ('Way of Ultimate Truth'), Chojiro Tani's **shukokai** ('Way for All'), and Shigeru Egami's **Shotokai** ('Shoto's Way').

How to find a good karate club

Unfortunately there are a great many poor quality karate clubs practising today, and there is no longer any easy way to discover where the good ones are. The first step is to obtain a list of karate clubs in your area. You can do this yourself by visiting your local sports centres and writing down the details of the clubs which advertise there.

Then go to the club on its training night and ask to be allowed to watch the training session. All good clubs will allow this and those which don't should be crossed off your list. The coach ought to look tidy and competent, and the class should seem disciplined, well ordered and interested.

Ask yourself whether the lesson is interesting in what it consists of and the way it is put across, and whether you would like to be in there with them training.

After the session, ask the coach whether he holds a National Coaching Foundation award, and whether students are covered by individual insurance. If the answer to both these questions is 'yes', then you may well have found a good local club. But just to help you make doubly sure, in the back of this book I have included some names and addresses of people who will be able to advise you further.

How much does training cost?

Karate is not an expensive activity to take up, though you will have to spend some money at the outset. Don't buy a karate suit straight away – wear a teeshirt and tracksuit bottoms until you're sure you are going to stick to it. When the time comes to buy your karate suit, ask the coach whether the club can get you one at a discounted price. Start off with a lightweight suit that's a size too large, because all tunics shrink every time they are washed. Expect to pay between £25–£35 for a good suit.

Check with the coach on the starting belt colour – it will either be red or white, depending upon the style. White belts are supplied with the suit and even if you begin on red, keep the white belt because you will need it after your first grading examination.

INTRODUCTION

Wrap the belt twice around your middle and adjust it until the two free ends are of equal length. Tuck the left-hand end under both turns of the belt, then bring it down and over the top of the brought forward right end. Tuck it through the right free end and pull the belt tight.

If you have tied the belt correctly, then the ends will be of equal length, and protrude from the knot in a 'quarter-to-three' position (Figure 1). If the free ends protrude in a 'quarter-to-six' position, then you have tucked the wrong end through the knot.

Figure 1   Tie your belt correctly and the belt ends will emerge from the knot in the quarter-to-three position.

INTRODUCTION

You will pay a nightly mat fee each time you train. This can vary between 50 pence and £3. There may also be an annual affiliation fee to be paid and if so, check that it includes the cost of a licence and record book. The licence is simply your individual membership receipt and proves that you are affiliated to a karate school. Some licences include the bonus of a valuable personal accident/third party indemnity – check this with your coach. The record book contains details of your training history. Annual registration fees vary between £5–£25 per year.

Expect to train twice a week, for about 90 minutes a session. Every month or so, the club will hold weekend training sessions, and sometimes a senior coach will visit the club to teach selected parts of the training syllabus. These sessions cost between £2.50 and £15, though sometimes they are free.

You will be invited to take a grading examination after training for around three months. This is a way of measuring how well you are progressing and each time you succeed you can wear a different belt colour. These coloured belt stages are known as **kyu** grades.

This is a typical sequence of belt colours:

> Red   White   Yellow   Orange   Green   Purple
> Brown (three stages)   Black

There are also stages within the black belt known as **dan** grades. The most qualified karate people in Britain are between fifth and seventh dan.

Grading examinations can cost anything from nothing, way up to as much as £50 for the black belt grading!

How to behave in the class

Karate classes are run in a disciplined way and the coach, known as **sensei**, must be obeyed without question at all times. Senior graded students must also be treated with respect.

Pause before you enter the training hall, place the palms of your hands on the front of your thighs and incline your upper body forwards in a standing bow. Keep your eyes on the coach the whole time. Pause briefly at the lowest point and then return to a standing position once more.

If the coach isn't present, then bow instead to the class senior. But if you are the first to arrive, then simply bow towards the centre of the empty room. Having done that, you can take off your shoes and enter the training hall.

INTRODUCTION

Begin to limber up, moving your arms, legs and trunk in a gradually increasing tempo as you prepare yourself for the rigours of training. Try and get yourself to the point where you feel warm, and then maintain that level until the class is called to order.

Look around for other people of your grade and line up with them. Straighten your karate suit and stand to attention with your heels together and your palms flat against your thighs.

On the command **'seiza!'**, drop smoothly down on to your right knee, bring the left to it and kneel down with your back straight. Your hands remain on the front of your thighs. The next command will be **'sensei ni rei!'**, meaning 'bow to the teacher!'. When you hear this, lean forward and slide your hands to the mat in front of your knees, so the fingertips touch. Although you bow quite low, you must always keep your eyes on the coach. Pause at the lowest position, then return to a straight-backed position once more.

The third command is **'otogai ni rei!'**, meaning that you should bow to those with whom you will train. Finally you will be told **'kiritsu!'**, meaning 'stand up!' Just reverse the original order of kneeling down and make a standing bow to complete the formal courtesy ritual. This ritual is repeated at the end of the training session.

Sometimes while you are kneeling, you may hear the command **'mokuso!'**. This means 'meditation', and you should simply close your eyes and visualise something soothing, such as a stream of running water. Meditation is used both to calm the mind and to concentrate your thoughts on the training to come.

You are now about to begin the week's training!

MONDAY

GETTING STARTED

Making a fist

The week's training begins by learning how to make the basic karate fist. To do this:

- open your hand out fully;

- fold down the fingers until they touch the bar of flesh running along the top of the palm;

- close the fist and lock the index and middle fingers by folding the thumb across (Figure 2).

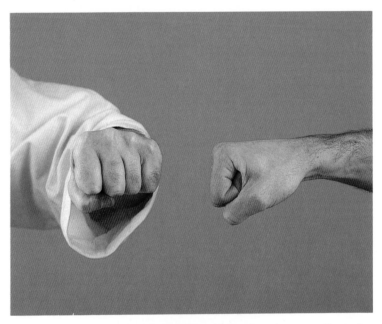

Figure 2   Close your fist fully and fold the thumb across the index and middle fingers.

Now look at your fist. Your knuckles are uneven and it is obvious that you cannot land with equal impact on all of them. This is why karate punches use only the index and middle finger knuckles. There is another advantage to using just two knuckles which is that it concentrates the force of impact through a small area, making your punches more effective.

MONDAY

Use an impact pad made from several layers of dense plastic foam to check that you are striking with the correct knuckles. Step forward with your left leg and pull your right fist back to your side. Extend your left hand forwards and turn your hips, so they are about 45° away from the pad and the person holding it. Then do three things all at once:

- twist your hips towards the pad;
- pull your left arm back;
- punch the pad lightly with your right fist (Figure 3).

You will probably find that you can't fold your fingers tight enough, so the fist hits the pad with the middle knuckles. Don't worry – this is a common

Figure 3   Turn your hips forward and punch the pad, trying to land just with the knuckles of the index and middle finger.

fault and will be corrected either by repeated pad work or by press-ups on closed fists from a cushioned surface.

Pad work also teaches you how to angle your wrist joint, so it doesn't flex or twist on hard impact. You will discover that the best impacts are made when the supporting bones of the two leading knuckles are in one straight line, through the wrist, with the two bones in the forearm.

Trouble Shooting

Problems	Resolutions
Your wrist flexes downwards on impact with the pad.	You hit the pad with your knuckles low.
Your wrist flexes outwards on impact.	You hit the pad with your knuckles turned to one side.
Your lower three knuckles become red after using the pad.	You are hitting the pad with the wrong knuckles. Use only index and middle knuckles.
The middle joints of your fingers become red.	You aren't closing your fist tightly enough. Keep working on the pad.
You hurt your thumb on impact.	Check that you aren't folding your thumb inside your fingers, or that it isn't poking forward.

Most karate punches use a twisting action of the forearm, so the fist turns palm-downwards as contact is made, but don't bother with this when punching the pad.

Holding your fist tightly slows the punch and soon tires the forearm muscles. Avoid this by closing the fist firmly – but not tightly – and tighten it only as it is about to make impact with the pad. The sudden spasm of the forearm muscles caused by clenching the fist makes it feel heavier and adds to its impact.

Don't worry if your knuckles become reddened through pad work. This is normal. But avoid punching so hard and so often that the joints become swollen and sore. Stop punching if this happens and switch to another part of the training schedule until the swelling has subsided.

MONDAY

Punches

Basic punch

Once you can make a good fist, the next step is learning how to throw it. Begin from a feet apart stance by stepping to the side first with the left foot, then with the right, until both are approximately a shoulder-width apart. Twist your feet slightly outwards. Draw your right fist back to the hip and turn it palm-upwards. Extend your left hand and turn it palm forward. Your extended hand is in the mid-line of the body (Figure 4).

Figure 4   Extend your left hand and pull the right fist back to your hip.

To perform the punch:

* withdraw your left hand and close it into a fist. Simultaneously thrust out the right, so they pass each other at the mid-way point (Figure 5);

* rotate both fists just before impact so the right fist turns palm-down and the left, palm-upwards (Figure 6). This action **must** be simultaneous;

Figure 5   Your fists travel at equal speed, so they pass each other at the mid-way point.

Figure 6   Rotate and clench both fists simultaneously as the punch is about to strike.

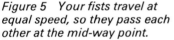

● keep both fists relaxed until now, then clench them tightly as imaginary impact occurs.

You have now performed a single punch. Make ready to perform a second by relaxing your shoulders and drawing back your right fist, whilst extending your open left hand once more. Perform the punch up to 10 times on one side, then change over and practise punching with your left fist.

Always keep your shoulders square-on to the front and don't allow the punching arm to drag the shoulder behind it. Having said that, a certain amount of shoulder movement is essential to make the punch more powerful. Therefore pull your shoulder back slightly as you withdraw a fist, then twist it forward a few degrees as that same fist extends – but do not exaggerate the movement. Allow the shoulders to drop slightly as the punching arm reaches full extension because this locks the arm and gives it extra rigidity.

Use hip action to further increase the power of your punch by first withdrawing the hip and fist together, then by twisting the hip forward a few degrees as that same fist extends. Do not exaggerate this movement.

15

MONDAY

Trouble Shooting

Problems	Resolutions
Your shoulders hunch up as you punch.	Relax your shoulders and don't let them lift.
Your shoulders swing behind each punch.	Restrict shoulder action to a few degrees of movement. Concentrate on pulling back the spent punch rather than on thrusting out the other.
The hips swing behind the punch.	Restrict hip action to a few degrees of movement. Use a short, whiplash action.
Your punch crosses the centre-line of your own body.	Power development is most efficient when your punch is made to the centre-line of your body.

The pulley principle

Let's now look at the punching action in a little more detail.

Most beginners concentrate only on the punch and ignore the pull-back of the extended hand. This produces an incorrect and unbalanced action and an ineffective punch. To get the feel of a correct punching action, take up your stance facing a firmly anchored pole. Pass your belt around it and grasp an end in each hand. Then adjust the length of belt held such that when one fist is extended, you have enough free play to pull the other end back to your hip.

Begin slowly by pulling back the withdrawing fist, rather than by thrusting out the punch. Because your arms are linked through the belt, they move at equal speeds and your fist shoots out, rather than is thrust out. Speed up the action as you become used to it and this will generate the right feel.

Multiple punches

Next we look at how to perform flurries of powerful punches using the pulley principle described above. Take up a straddle stance (also known as horse riding stance) by stepping to the side with left and right feet until they are about half as wide again as the shoulders. Either point your feet forwards or turn them slightly inwards. Bend your knees to nearly a right angle and keep your back straight; neither leaning forward nor poking your backside out.

MONDAY

This is a very tiring stance and soon your thighs will begin to ache with the strain of holding it. By all means lift the stance slightly, or even lower it – but do not come out of it until the end of practice. This is because straddle stance is very good for strengthening the muscles which position the bones of the knee – and this is very important to safe kicking. Extend your left arm and twist the fist palm downwards in the mid-line of the body (Figure 7).

Figure 7   Practise multiple punches from a low straddle stance.
Extend your left arm and twist the fist palm-downwards.

MONDAY

The Kiai

Now is the time to add yet more power to your punch by harnessing your breathing to the punching action. Take a quick intake of breath just before you punch, then expel it strongly and quickly as your fist thumps home. Some karate schools insist that you shape your exhalation into a loud 'EEEEH!'.

Kiai, as it is known, can be used together with any karate technique that involves powerful action coupled with determined execution.

To perform a series of punches:

- withdraw your left fist and simultaneously thrust out the right, so they pass each other at the midway point;

- rotate both fists simultaneously so the right turns palm down and the left, palm upwards. Clench them tightly on impact;

- immediately withdraw the right fist whilst punching with the left.

Aim each successive punch to a different height, the first into the imaginary opponent's face; the second into the groin; the third into the chest – but always keep your punch to the centre-line.

It is always better to punch slowly with good technique than quickly with bad form. Use a mirror to check the quality of your technique.

Trouble Shooting

Problems	Resolutions
The shoulders swing wildly behind successive punches.	This is a common fault. Restrict shoulder movement to a few degrees only.
The hips turn strongly behind successive punches.	As above, restrict hip movement to a few degrees.
The shoulders gradually lift.	Keep your shoulders relaxed.
The punches drift off centre.	Keep punches to the centre-line.
The punches blur into one another.	Complete each punch before beginning the next – but avoid jerkiness.

MONDAY

Blocks

Blocking techniques are used to deflect an attack. Sometimes moving out of the way is enough to make an attacking technique miss and in such cases the block then functions simply as insurance. At other times the block forms part of your counter-attack, closing the opponent off and preventing him from continuing his attack. Blocks can also double as attacks insofar as they can injure the opponent.

Head block

Head block uses a diagonal upwards/outwards rolling action of your forearm to deflect the opponent's face punch. The palm is turned to the floor during delivery, but as the block engages the attack, so the forearm rotates until the little finger-side of the fist faces upwards (Figure 8). The block intercepts the punch before it reaches the face and the twisting action bumps it upwards so it clears the head.

Figure 8   The blocking forearm travels diagonally upwards and outwards to meet the incoming punch. Roll your forearm until the little finger turns upwards.

MONDAY

Practise head block from a posture called 'hourglass stance'. Begin from the straddle stance shown in Figure 7 on page 17 by narrowing it and then advancing one foot so the heel is in line with the toes of the rear foot. Lift your hips and tilt the pelvis forwards so the groin is protected from a kick between the legs. Clench your buttocks and stiffen the upper legs, taking body weight on the outside edges of the feet (Figure 9).

Figure 9   Hourglass stance has the heel of the leading foot in line with the toes of the trailing foot. Both feet are turned inwards-facing.

Figure 10   Moving at equal speed, the two forearms momentarily form an x-block.

Figure 11   Draw the left arm powerfully back to the hip, using this action to thrust out the blocking forearm.

Pull your right hand back to the hip and extend the left upwards until the fist is well above and in front of the head. Rotate your forearm until the little finger points upwards. This is the starting position. To perform the block:

- twist your left fist and draw it down, close to your chest;

- overlay it with the advancing right arm which is moving at an equivalent speed, so a sort of 'X' shape results (Figure 10);

- use a strong pulley action, drawing the spent left arm back to the ribs as the right rises upwards and outwards (Figure 11).

21

MONDAY

Forearm rotation is important because it strengthens the block and improves the degree of deflection obtained. But don't forget, both arms rotate – not just one! Bring the crook in the elbow close to the side of your head and you will more easily resist attempts to smash the forearm down.

Practise head block with a partner. Take up hourglass stance whilst your partner uses straddle stance. Your partner then extends his left arm and adjusts range until his fist just reaches your forehead. Bring your right forearm up in a slow block to lift the punch clear of your face. Then your partner smoothly punches with his right fist whilst withdrawing the left. DO THIS SLOWLY! Withdraw your right arm and block with the left. Neither of you should lean forwards or backwards at any time.

Set the speed of practice so you can comfortably deflect the incoming punches. Only then can the speed of delivery slightly increase by mutual agreement. The object is to put you under pressure to improve your blocking skill without overloading your as yet meagre skills.

Trouble Shooting

Problems

You can't see the punch and your block deflects it into your forehead.

Your block connects with the punch but the latter strikes you before you can sweep it upwards.

Your block misses the punch.

Resolutions

Lift your blocking arm higher so it both clears your eyes and deflects the punch above your head.

You are blocking too close to your face. Take your block outwards, so it intercepts the punch further from your face.

Block across the front of your face, sweeping a wide area clear of incoming techniques.

Lower parry

Lower parry is used against a variety of straight attacks aimed at the lower stomach. Use the little finger side of your forearm in a diagonal wiping action across the front of the body that comes to rest about four inches above and slightly to the outside of the leading knee. Use this block with caution and ensure that it sweeps attacking techniques to the side, rather than meeting them full-on.

Do not attempt to block front kick by swinging your forearm into the path of a fast-moving shin!

MONDAY

Take up hourglass stance. Then:

- extend your left arm diagonally downwards and lift the palm of the right fist close to your left ear (Figure 12);

- wipe your right forearm down across the left as pulley action withdraws the left to the hip;

- extend your blocking arm as the withdrawing fist comes to rest palm upwards against the ribs;

- rotate your blocking forearm and pull your left hip back slightly to help the block unroll (Figure 13).

Figure 12   Bring your right fist close to your ear and extend the left arm diagonally forward and down.

Figure 13   Use pulley action to power the block and enhance this with hip action.

MONDAY

Practise a series of lower parries until you get the feel of the technique. Then take up a position facing your partner so he can reach your stomach with his fist. He begins punching slowly, first on one side then on the other. Block each punch with a lower parry and gradually build up speed as your confidence and skill increase.

Trouble Shooting

Problems	**Resolutions**
The opponent's punch is swept into the side of your stomach or hip.	You haven't swept the punch sufficiently clear of your body. Pull the opposite hip back slightly to aid deflection.
You block too far to the side, so your next block is delayed.	Block only so far as is necessary to ensure that the attack misses.
The opponent's punch slips in under your block.	You are blocking too high. Bring your forearm down, closer to your body.

Kicks

Front kick

A front kick thrusts the ball of the foot into the opponent's mid-section, but before you can even begin to try it you must learn how to pull your foot quickly into the correct shape. See what this feels like by raising your heel as high as possible from the floor, so the toes are flexed back and the instep is in line with the shin. Keep this shape as you raise your foot from the floor and point it at the target.

Work on the impact pad to develop both correct kicking action and foot shape. Beginners often don't pull their toes back, or they flex the ankle joint. The first fault leads to painful toe injuries; the second shortens the kick and makes it ineffective. Remember – do not use front kick until you can form a safe foot shape!

Practise front kick from a posture called 'forward stance'. Step forward a good pace and a half with your left foot and ensure it points forward. Bend your front knee until it is directly above the mid-section of the instep. Your rear leg functions as a prop, so fully straighten the knee and twist the rear foot until it is 45° from straight ahead.

The front and rear feet are not in line. Instead the front foot is stepped out by at least two fist-widths. Your hips and shoulders are turned 45°

MONDAY

from front-facing, the shoulders are relaxed and the head is erect. Hold both arms well away from your sides and clench the hands into fists.

Perform front kick by:

- raising the right foot and bringing the right hip forward. Keep the sole of your foot parallel to the floor;

- swinging your right knee forward and up, twisting your left foot outwards slightly. Keep your left knee slightly bent (Figure 14);

- raising your kicking knee until it is slightly above the height of the target, then thrusting the foot out (Figure 15);

Figure 14 Swing your kicking knee forward and up. Allow the supporting foot to twist outwards.

Figure 15 Your kicking knee drops slightly as the foot thrusts out.

MONDAY

- striking the impact pad with the ball of your foot, then promptly withdrawing the spent kick before the opponent can seize it and pull you off balance;

- bringing the spent kicking foot back to the side of your left knee and setting it back down in its original position once more.

Front kick uses a smooth, seamless action to accelerate the kick all the way from floor to target. The knee is always raised slightly higher than the target and it drops slightly as the foot thrusts out.

Trouble Shooting

Problems

Resolutions

Problems	Resolutions
Your groin opens as you lift the kicking foot.	The kicking foot must brush the side of the supporting knee both on the way out and during retrieval.
Your kick is too low.	Lift your kicking knee above the height of the target.
Your whole body bobs upwards as you perform the kick.	Keep your supporting leg bent as you kick and the supporting foot should be flat on the floor.
Your shoulders hunch up as you kick.	Keep your shoulders relaxed and your arms still.
Your kick is off-centre.	Aim the kick into your centre-line.
You fall forward after the kick.	Control your centre of gravity by leaning back.
Impact on the pad sends you backwards and off balance.	You leaned back too far!

Roundhouse kick

This kick can be made either with the ball of the foot, or with the toes pointing and using the top of the foot. We will consider the former version. As its name implies, the roundhouse kick travels a horizontal, circular path, striking the target from the side. Use it to attack the ribs, or side of jaw. Begin from left forward stance:

- lift your right foot, pull the toes back, twist outwards on your left foot;

- raise your right knee, bringing it forwards and to the side in one smooth movement (Figure 16);

Figure 16   Raise your right knee to the side.

Figure 17   Swivel on your supporting foot until the kicking knee is right across your body.

- continue twisting on your left foot until your right knee is brought across the front of the body. The supporting leg has turned outwards at least 90° by this stage (Figure 17);

27

- thrust your right foot out horizontally as the knee reaches the height of the target (Figure 18);

Figure 18
Thrust your foot
out in a
horizontal arc.

- hit the target, then pull your foot back before the opponent can grab hold of it;

- withdraw the kicking hip and return the right foot to its original position.

One of the best ways to practise roundhouse kick is to turn your upper body and take hold of a chair back with both hands. This encourages you to turn your shoulders first, then your hips as you perform the kick. The more your shoulders turn, the more powerful the kick becomes.

MONDAY

Trouble Shooting

Problems	Resolutions
The kicking foot follows a diagonal rather than a horizontal path.	You have not turned your hips sufficiently and raised your kicking knee to the correct height.
The knee turns downwards as the kick is performed.	You have tried to kick higher than your present level of hip flexibility will allow.
The kicking foot does not tense on impact.	Pull your foot into the correct shape and stiffen your ankle.
You fall forward as the kick is delivered.	Keep control over your centre of gravity by leaning back. Hold on to a chair back until the movement becomes familiar.

Some faults associated with front kick also occur in roundhouse kick, so re-read the appropriate section and see how many common faults you can identify.

BASIC TECHNIQUES ON THE MOVE

Punching on the move

Yesterday you practised punching whilst standing still. Today you will learn how to punch on the move.

Begin from attention stance by stepping out with your left leg, then your right, until both feet are about a shoulder-width apart. Now close your fists and let your arms hang naturally at your sides (Figure 19). This is 'ready stance'. Then step back a good pace-and-a-half with your right leg and bring your left arm down in a lower parry. At the same time, draw your right fist back to your right hip and turn it palm upwards facing (Figure 20).

Figure 19   Stand erect, relax your shoulders and let your arms hang naturally at your sides. Close your hands into fists.

Figure 20   Step forward a good pace and a half, so the back leg is straight and the front knee overlies the instep.

You are now in forward stance. Use a mirror to check that:

- your leading left foot points straight ahead;
- your left knee is directly above your instep;
- your left fist is just above and to the outside of your knee;
- your shoulders are relaxed;
- your right fist lies just above the right hip;
- your right elbow is tucked well back and not flapping at your side;
- your right hip is pulled back 45° from forward-facing;
- your right knee is fully extended so the leg is locked straight;
- your right foot points 45° from forward-facing.

Lunge punch

Perform lunge punch from left forward stance (see Figure 20 again). Then:

- turn your left foot outwards slightly;
- step swiftly forward with your right foot (Figure 21);

- continue on forward with your right foot until it is a pace-and-a-half in front of the left;
- just as weight settles on your right heel, pull back your left fist and thrust out the right. Time the movements so your punching fist rotates palm downwards as your left fist turns palm upwards on your hip.

You are now in right forward stance, with your right fist leading and your left hip pulled back 45°.

Figure 21 Step forward but keep your knees bent, so you don't bob up and down.

31

TUESDAY

Trouble Shooting

Problems	Resolutions
Your step forward feels awkward.	Did you turn your leading foot outwards before you stepped?
Your new stance is higher than the original.	You did not step forward far enough.
Your new stance is lower and more stretched-out than the original.	You stepped forward too far.
Your new stance feels unstable in a side-to-side direction.	You brought your foot inwards as you stepped forward and your new stance is too narrow.
Your new stance is too wide.	You moved your foot outwards as you stepped forward.
There's little weight on your front foot and your lead knee is not well bent.	You haven't moved your body weight far enough forward.
Your lead knee overlies your toes.	You have moved your body weight too far forward.
Your rear knee is bent.	Straighten it fully.
Your rear foot faces 90° away from forward facing.	Turn it to 45° from forward or your punch will lack power.
Your shoulders hunch up as you step.	Keep your shoulders relaxed or your punch will suffer.
You bob up and down as you step.	Keep your supporting leg bent during the step.
Your cocked fist moves away from your hip as you step.	Hold the fist lightly but firmly against your hip.
Your extended arm waves about as you step.	Keep your extended arm still.
The punching action throws you forwards and off balance.	You punched too early during the step.
The punching action feels too weak.	You punched too late, when forward body movement had come to a stop.

32

TUESDAY

Repeat the stepping action several times, punching each time your forward body movement comes to a stop. Eventually you will run out of space. When this happens, go on to the following section.

Turn and head block

Let's assume that you are in left forward stance when you run out of space. Now follow the sequence:

- look over your right shoulder to check that it is safe to turn;
- step straight across in a clockwise direction with your right foot, keeping your knee bent and your heel clear of the floor (Figure 22);
- twist your hips towards the right and bend your left elbow, so your fist covers your face (Figure 23);

Figure 22   Step sharply across with your trailing foot. Both knees are bent and the heel of the moving foot is lifted clear of the floor.

Figure 23   Turn sharply about-face and bend your left elbow so the forearm acts as an interim block.

*Figure 24   Pull back
your left fist and block
with the right forearm.*

- pull back your left fist, thrusting your right diagonally across the front of your chest (Figure 24);

- your left fist comes to rest on your hip as your right reaches up and forwards into head block.

Only experience and good coaching will teach you how far to step across with your trailing foot. It may help to imagine that there is a line reaching back from your leading heel. Think of this as the centre-line for the turn. Then if you have stepped the correct distance, your trailing foot will move an equal distance to the other side of the centre-line.

Always step across on the ball of your trailing foot and keep both knees well bent.

> **Trouble Shooting**
>
> | Problems | Resolutions |
> |---|---|
> | Your new stance is too wide. | You stepped across the centre-line too far. |
> | Your new stance is too narrow. | You didn't step far enough across the centre-line. |
> | Your new stance is too high. | You brought your foot in towards you as you stepped across. |
> | You bobbed up and down as you turned. | You straightened your knees as you stepped across. |

Practise the turn/block several times, turning each way alternately. Aim to develop a smooth acceleration throughout the movement.

Reverse punch

Begin from left forward stance and lower parry. On the command 'Punch without stepping forward!', simply draw back your left arm and punch strongly with the right (Figure 25). A strong punching action will cause the right hip to move forward from a trailing 45° angle until both hips are square-on. Help this action by allowing:

- your left foot to slide diagonally back and outwards;
- your right foot to twist so it comes to face forwards.

Two imaginary lines drawn through your feet would therefore intersect at some distance in front of the stance.

Figure 25   Punch without stepping forwards, so the opposite fist and foot now lead.

Compare reverse punch with forward stance and see whether you can pick out the important differences.

Step forward and perform a reverse punch on the move by:

- turning your left foot slightly outwards (this helps the step through);

- bringing your right foot forwards and in, in a fast shallow arc (Figure 26);

Figure 26   Use a semicircular step to advance forward, bringing the trailing foot inwards.

- stepping past your left foot and skimming forwards and out in a continuation of the arc;

- withdrawing your right fist and punching with your left just as body weight moves forward behind the action.

If everything has gone well, then:

- your right foot and left fist now lead;

- your left hip is turned square-on;

- your right foot is turned inwards slightly and your left faces forward.

Although you are stepping in a shallow 'U', the step must be no slower than the direct move which you used in lunge punch.

Trouble Shooting

Read the remarks for lunge punch again and in addition, check the following:

Problems	Resolutions
Your final stance is too wide.	You stepped too far outwards.
Your final stance is too narrow.	You didn't step far enough outwards and lost side step.
Your front foot has turned outwards.	You haven't used your hips correctly.

TUESDAY

Reverse punch is probably the most commonly used technique in karate, so it is essential that you practise to get it right at the outset.

Continue practising reverse punch until you run out of space, then go on to the next section.

Turn and lower parry

Let's assume that you are in left reverse punch stance with your right fist leading when you run out of space. Now follow the sequence:

- look over your right shoulder to check that it is safe to turn;
- step straight across with your right foot, keeping your knee bent and your heel clear of the floor;
- bend your right elbow so the little finger of your right fist rests lightly against your left collar bone (Figure 27);
- twist your hips towards the right;
- sweep downwards with your right fist as you perform lower parry;
- pull back your right fist as you thrust the left forward in a reverse punch.

Figure 27   Fold the blocking arm across your chest as you turn.

If all has gone well, then your right foot and left fist should now be leading.

As you turn into the lower parry, you will find yourself in forward stance, leading with the right foot and right fist. Your left hip will be pulled 45° degrees back. But when you punch, your stance will of course change as the hip engages.

To trouble shoot with this sequence, check both the previous turn/head block, and the earlier description of lower parry.

TUESDAY

The mid-section forearm blocks

These two blocks use the thumb side of your forearm (the 'inside') and the little finger side (the 'outside') to sweep incoming techniques to the side. You will need a partner to see how they work.

Inner block

Face your partner in ready stance. He steps back with his left foot into forward stance/lower parry but you remain waiting. Then he steps forward and attempts to strike you in the chest with lunge punch. Even as he begins to step, you:

- step back with your right leg into forward stance;

- drop your left forearm palm downwards across your stomach (Figure 28);

- let your right fist move forward from your hip;

- pull your right fist back to the hip and draw your right hip back until it faces 45° from straight ahead;

- swing your left forearm upwards so it finishes with the fist at the same level as your shoulders, and with a 90° degree angle at the elbow;

- rotate your left forearm as it covers the last few degrees of arc, so the palm turns back towards you (Figure 29). This action brings the blocking action to an abrupt end.

Perform steps two through to six as you are stepping back – not once you have finished moving.

If you have timed things correctly, your forearm will swing upwards across the path of the opponent's punch and deflect it across his body.

Figure 28   Whilst you drop your left forearm down and across your body, partly extend your right fist.

The power for this block is generated by the pull-back of the right fist and hip. Develop maximum effect by bending your right elbow a full 90° and keeping it close to the ribs as you block.

Figure 29   Draw back your right fist and swing the left up like a windscreen wiper.

Trouble Shooting

Problems	Resolutions
The opponent punches you in the chest before you manage to step back.	Begin your step back as the opponent begins his advance.
The opponent steps on your toes as he advances.	You began too close to each other, or you didn't step back far enough.
You can't reach the opponent's punch with your block.	You began too far away from each other, or you took too long a step back.
The punch goes over the top of your blocking fist.	Your blocking forearm is not high enough, or the opponent has punched above chest height.
Your block deflects the punch into your shoulder.	You haven't blocked far enough across your body, you blocked too late or your left elbow moved away from your ribs.

TUESDAY

Having blocked the opponent, you can then pull your left arm back strongly, using this to help power a right reverse punch to his ribs. Notice that you have closed his punching arm across his body and made it impossible for him to counter punch you (Figure 30).

Practise this block and counter-punch 10 times, then try the block and counter-punch on the opposite side. This means that your partner first steps back with his right leg, and then lunge punches with his right fist. You step back with your left foot and block with your right arm.

Training with a partner in this way is useful because in addition to teaching you how to block a real punch, it also introduces you to the concepts of timing and distance.

Figure 30   Blocking in this way closes the opponent off and prevents him from counter attacking.

TUESDAY

Outer block

Figure 31 Bring your left fist to the side of your head and allow the right to move forward slightly.

Figure 32 Draw back the right fist to your hip and block across the front of your body with the left.

As before, your partner steps back with his right foot into forward stance/ lower parry whilst you remain waiting. Then he steps forward and attempts to strike you in the chest with lunge punch. But as he begins to step, you:

- step back with your right leg into forward stance;

- bring your left fist to the side of your left ear (Figure 31);

- let your right fist move forward from your hip;

- pull your right fist back to the hip and draw your right hip back until it faces 45° from straight ahead;

- swing your left forearm forwards across your chest, keeping the elbow bent at 90° so the fist is at the same level as your shoulders;

- rotate your forearm as it travels the last few degrees of arc, so the knuckles turn away from you (Figure 32).

TUESDAY

As before, perform steps two through to six as you are stepping back – not once you have finished moving. And if you have timed things correctly, your forearm will swing horizontally across the path of the opponent's punch and deflect it outwards.

Outside block is powered by the same mechanism as inner block but now it is even more important to bring your blocking elbow close to your ribs. The twisting of the forearm and the clenching of the fist near the end of the blocking action ensures a more efficient deflection.

Complete the block with a reverse punch, using the pull-back of your spent block to power the counter-punch. Practise this block on both sides.

Trouble Shooting

The problems you get with inner and outer block are similar except for the following:

Problems	Resolutions
The punch gets knocked down into the side of your stomach.	You didn't use a horizontal blocking action and/or your blocking elbow moved away from your ribs.
It took a long time to counter punch.	You carried your block too far across.

Kicking on the move

Front kick

Step back with your right foot into left forward stance and hold your arms away from your sides. Then bring your right knee forwards and up as you perform front kick to an imaginary opponent's mid-section.

First pull your spent foot back, so the opponent can't take hold of it, then land forward with your right foot and take up a forwards stance once more.

Perform front kick again but this time with your left leg. Continue performing kicks on each leg until you run out of space, then look over your shoulder and turn sharply about face (see Turning pages 33–34).

Keep control over your centre of gravity as you kick, so you can set your spent kicking foot down carefully, instead of having to slap it down. The opponent could be waiting to sweep your foot away, so you must always be able to withdraw it.

TUESDAY

Roundhouse kick

Begin from left forward stance, bringing your right knee up and across your front. Pivot on your supporting leg and perform roundhouse kick to mid-section. Bring your spent kick back and then set it down carefully so you finish up in a right forward stance. Then repeat the kick on each leg alternately until you run out of space.

Two new kicks

Side kick

Side kick is a powerful thrusting kick that is delivered with the heel and little toe edge of the foot. Begin practice by getting the correct foot shape. Straighten your leg and pull the big toe side of your foot towards you, so the little toe edge leads. Then lift your big toe and turn the others down.

You must get this shape exactly right, otherwise you may find that you are kicking with the sole of your foot – and this wastes energy and makes the kick less effective.

Begin the kick from ready stance, using the following sequence:

● look to your right;

● lean slightly to the left and lift your right foot off the ground;

● raise your right knee and form your foot into the correct shape;

● twist your left foot to the left and point your kicking heel at an imaginary opponent's mid-section (Figure 33);

Figure 33 Lift your heel until it is pointing at the target.

Figure 34   Thrust out your right foot like a piston.

- thrust out your right foot like a piston whilst twisting further to the left on your left foot (Figure 34);

- withdraw the spent kick by bringing the foot close to your left thigh, then set it down carefully.

The power for an effective side kick comes from a combination of the twisting action on the support foot plus a thrusting action of the kicking leg. But the kick must first be 'cocked' and that is done by turning away from the target.

You must lean back, or the energy of your kicking leg will draw you forwards. Keep control over your arms and don't allow them to wave about.

Practise 10 side kicks with the right leg, then switch to the left for 10 more.

Trouble Shooting

Problems	Resolutions
The kick is low.	You didn't lift your kicking knee high enough.
You lose balance in the direction of the kick.	You didn't lean back far enough.
The kick lacks power.	You didn't succeed in co-ordinating the twist on your supporting foot with the thrusting out of the kick.

The main problem with side kick is generally lack of hip flexibility. If this is the case, then aim your kick at an imaginary opponent's knee cap. Always try to make your kick technically correct and your body will learn the feel of a good technique. Then when hip flexibility improves, you will be able to raise the height of the kick gradually.

Back kick

Think of back kick as a fairly extreme form of side kick. Begin from a left forward stance and follow the sequence:

● look over your left shoulder to sight the target;

● bring your left knee up and back (Figure 35);

Figure 35 Look at the target as you bring your left knee back and up.

- thrust your left heel directly back into the target (Figure 36) but snap it back again before putting it down to the ground.

It helps if you bring your elbows close to your sides.

Practise the kick 10 times, then switch sides and do 10 more.

Figure 36   Keep watching the target as you thrust your heel directly back and into the target.

WEDNESDAY

PRACTICAL TECHNIQUES IN ACTION

Punching techniques

Snap punch

Begin snap punch from left forward stance, with your left arm extended into lower parry and the right held against the hip. Then:

- step swiftly forward into right forward stance;
- draw back your left fist and use this to help power a fast punch into the opponent's face with the right fist;
- withdraw the spent punching fist to a forward guard position immediately after it makes contact with the imaginary opponent (Figure 37).

The forward guard position carries the leading fist at shoulder height, with the elbow bent 90° and held close to the ribs. Your rear guard hand sits palm-upwards on the hip, as before.

Figure 37   Withdraw snap punch into a forward guard position.

Repeat the snap punch on alternate sides as you take a series of steps forward. When you eventually run out of space, look over your shoulder, slide your rear foot across and about-face. Even as you turn, bring your leading guard across your body and then pull it back to the hip as the new lead hand swings upwards and out in the manner of an inner block (pages 38–39).

Reverse punch with pull back

Begin from a left forward stance, with your left arm extended into a lower parry. Then:

- sharply pull back your left arm whilst punching with the right;
- twist your right hip forward, so both hips face square-on;
- allow your front foot to move naturally back and outwards, and your rear foot to turn forwards;
- then pull your punch back to the right hip, using this action to help drive forward your left leading guard hand;
- draw back your right hip and allow your feet to return to forward stance position.

This punch uses a double pulley action, the first being the drawing back of the lower parry to power the punch, and the second being the pulling back of the spent punch to drive forward the guard hand.

Practise this punch on both sides, then try it again from a fighting stance. Fighting stance (Figure 38) has the following characteristics:

- it is shorter than forward stance, being about a good pace in length;
- it has the same width as forward stance;
- body weight is carried equally over both feet;
- both knees are flexed, so as to give the stance a certain springiness.

Figure 38   Fighting stance is a highly mobile posture with a realistic guard.

WEDNESDAY

Fighting stance is used a great deal during sparring and kicking. Because it is higher than forward stance, it allows you to move more quickly, and because body weight is spread 50–50 over the feet, you can move equally well in all directions.

Begin from a left fighting stance and:

- push forward with your right leg;

- allow the front foot to skim forward a short distance;

- pull back your lead guard hand, using this action to power a fast reverse punch;

- withdraw your spent punch to the hip and reinstate your leading guard hand;

- draw up your rear foot to prevent the stance from elongating.

Striking techniques

Back fist

Whereas the normal punch uses the front of the index and middle knuckles, back fist strikes with their upper surface. To perform back fist:

- take up left fighting stance;

- bring your leading fist back and down, so the thumb presses against your stomach and the elbow points at the opponent's face (Figure 39);

Figure 39   Point your elbow at your opponent's jaw.

49

- pull your right hip back, using this action to help 'unroll' your left elbow, so your fist lifts and moves along a circular path into the side of the opponent's jaw;

- rotate your fist sharply as impact is about to be made, so the upper part of the knuckles strikes the target (Figure 40);

- bring the spent fist sharply back to a forward guard position and return your hips to a 45° position once more.

Back fist is a fast technique which relies upon a whiplash action of the elbow and wrist joints to deliver a sharp impact. It is quite a long-range hand technique – it will out-range a reverse punch, for example, but it is not so powerful as a linear punch.

Figure 40   Your hips turn away as the arm unrolls into the target.

Hammer fist

We have already come across hammer fist in the form of the lower parry and outer forearm block. These bat an incoming technique to one side, using the little finger edge of the rolled fist to administer the deflection. But you can also use hammer fist as a strike. The opponent first steps back into left forward stance/lower parry. Then he advances into right forward stance and attempts to grasp your lapel. As he does so:

- step diagonally back with your left leg;
- bend your left elbow so the forearm is across your chest;
- bring your right arm up so the fist is just behind your ear (Figure 41);

Figure 41 Bring your right fist behind and above your right ear.

Figure 42   Strike down onto the opponent's collar bone with the base of your fist.

● draw back your left fist, using this action to power a swinging downwards strike to the opponent's collar bone (Figure 42).

You do not step directly back with your left leg; rather you set yourself up on the diagonal. Bring your left arm forward even as you are stepping and try to complete the strike as you settle into the new stance.

WEDNESDAY

Blocking techniques

Knife block

Knife block uses the little finger edge of the hand to deflect a punch or strike. Get the correct hand shape by extending your fingers and folding the thumb across the palm. To practise knife block, you need to learn a new posture known as 'back stance' (Figure 43). This has the following characteristics:

Figure 43 Move back over your rear leg until it is bearing 75 per cent of the weight.

- back stance is about as long as fighting stance;
- it has no sidestep, so both heels lie in one line;
- 75 per cent of body weight is borne on the rear foot and only 25 per cent on the front foot;
- the trailing knee is well bent, the leading knee less so;
- the hips and shoulders are turned a full 90° away from forwards facing;
- the lead knee faces forwards and the rear points out at 90°.

Practise stepping back into back stance from ready stance, alternating left and right leading legs.

WEDNESDAY

To practise knife block, take up ready stance as the opponent faces you in right forward stance. Even as he steps forward and punches:

● step back into back stance with your left foot forward;

● extend your right hand forward, turning the palm down to the floor;

● bring your left hand around so it almost cups your right ear (Figure 44);

Figure 44   Your left hand almost cups your right ear and the right projects forwards.

● pull your right hand back and turn it palm upwards in front of your chest;

● pull your right shoulder back;

● cut outwards with your left hand, so the little finger edge catches the opponent's wrist (Figure 45).

Pulling back the right arm and shoulder provides power for the block. And twisting your left forearm to present the palm forwards also adds sharpness to it.

Practise by stepping back again from your partner's second attack, this time blocking with the edge of your right hand.

*Figure 45   Draw back your right hand and rotate it palm-upwards.
Use this action to help power the knife block.*

Trouble Shooting

Problems
The punch hits you before you have chance to block.

Your knife block is too weak.

Resolutions
Knife block is difficult to learn so get your partner to slow down.

Have you pulled back your right hand sharply enough? Did you turn your hips away from the blocking action? Did you twist your forearm just before you contacted the punch?

Scooping block

Scooping block is performed together with a strong twisting motion of the hips that takes the body out of harm's way. The opponent faces you in left forward stance and aims a front kick to your mid-section. You begin from left fighting stance and even as his kicking foot lifts off the floor:

- step outwards with your left foot;

- twist your hips strongly towards the right, so both feet swivel;

- bring your left hand around and under the opponent's calf, lifting and deflecting his front kick (Figure 46);

Figure 46   Turn your hips and scoop the opponent's heel with your left hand.

Figure 47   Turn your hips back and reverse punch the opponent.

- twist your hips forwards once more, withdraw your left arm and perform reverse punch with your right fist into the back of the opponent's head, or into his kidneys (Figure 47).

The opening sidestep and hip twist are important because they take your body out of the line of the kick. Practise until you can avoid and scoop even a full power kick.

Trouble Shooting

Problems	Resolutions
The opponent's kick caught you in the hip.	You didn't side step with your leading foot. Also you did not twist your hips sharply enough.
Your block was weak.	Twist your hips more powerfully.
Your punch was weak.	Twist your hips back towards the opponent.

The most common fault is not turning your hips fully, so you only turn side-on to the opponent.

Kicking on the move

Side kick

Begin from left fighting stance. Then follow the sequence:

- change your guard hands over and twist your left foot outwards;
- bring your right knee forward and up, so it comes across the front of your body;
- twist your hips so your back is almost towards the opponent;
- point your heel directly at the target (Figure 48);
- thrust your foot out like a piston, turning your hips further away as you do so (Figure 49);

Figure 48   Lift your foot until the heel points at the target . . .

Figure 49   . . . then thrust it out in a straight line.

- extend your right arm along your body and fold the left against your chest;

- twist your hips back around to the front and withdraw the spent kick. Then set it down.

Side kick off the back leg is extremely difficult because it combines a rotational movement of the body with a straight thrusting movement of the leg.

Trouble Shooting

Problems	**Resolutions**
The kick is weak and lacks penetration.	You have failed to twist your hips away as you thrust the foot out.
The spent kick drags you forwards and off balance.	You failed to twist your hips back whilst withdrawing your foot.

Back kick

Begin from a left fighting stance. Then:

- slide your left foot across to the right;
- twist your hips and rotate your head clockwise;
- transfer weight to your left leg and pick up the right (Figure 50);
- lift your right knee then thrust your right heel back and into the target (Figure 51);

Figure 51   Thrust your right heel directly back and into the target.

Figure 50   Look at the target and raise your right foot, bringing the knee close to your body.

Figure 52   Set your foot down with your hips still partly turned.

- partly withdraw the spent foot, then drop it to the side (Figure 52);
- turn into right fighting stance.

Take your eyes away from the target for the shortest of time intervals and work at the kick until the step across, turn and kick become one smooth movement.

Trouble Shooting

Problems
Your kick goes either side of the centre.

Resolutions
You either didn't slide your lead foot far enough across, or you moved it too far.

Your foot hooks upwards as you kick.

Drop and withdraw your foot as the kick completes.

61

PUTTING TECHNIQUES TOGETHER

A new strike to learn

Elbow

The elbow is a devastating short range weapon. It can be used in a number of different ways of which this is the most common:

- take up left fighting stance;
- draw back your leading guard hand;
- twist your hips around until they are square-on;
- bring your elbow up and around in a rising circular strike that clips the opponent's jaw (Figure 53).

Hit the target with the tip of your elbow, not your forearm.

Figure 53   Use your hips and pull back the left fist to power the elbow strike.

Figure 54   Extend your left hand and fold the right across your chest.

You can also use elbow in a slightly different way. Begin from left fighting stance and:

- look over your right shoulder;

- slide your back foot around until both heels are in line;

- reach across your stomach with your open left hand;

- take your right arm across your chest with the palm facing downwards (Figure 54);

Figure 55   Step across the front of your supporting foot.

- then swivel your hips a further 45°, so you are in a straddle stance, with knees bent equally;

- pull your left hand back to your ribs and thrust your right elbow out and into the opponent (Figure 55).

Practise the various stages until they run smoothly together.

THURSDAY

Kicking techniques

One step kicks

Sometimes the opponent is out of range of your kick, in which case you can close distance quickly with a scissors step. Begin from left fighting stance and:

- take a step forward with the rear foot, turning the toes outwards (Figure 56);
- then perform a front or roundhouse kick with the trailing foot.

Keep your guard steady as you skim the advancing foot over the ground. Adjust the length of the step to suit the distance to be covered, and don't straighten your knees as you advance, or you will bob up and down.

Figure 56   Keep your guard up as you step forward.

Figure 57   Stepping behind the supporting foot sets up the hips for a side kick.

In most cases, your advancing foot skims across the front of the shin of the supporting leg, but there is one case where it passes behind the supporting leg (Figure 57). It so happens that stepping in this particular way sets up the hips for an excellent side kick.

Double kicks

A good test of kicking ability is to be able to perform two kicks on the same leg, without setting the foot down in between. Begin from a left fighting stance and:

● perform a half-speed roundhouse kick to the opponent's mid-section;

- withdraw the kick smoothly;

- lean back and swivel your supporting foot a little more;

- perform a second roundhouse kick, this time to the opponent's head.

The double kick works this way because the lower kick uses only part of the supporting foot's available swivel, leaving the rest to be used up by the head kick.

Practise this kick whilst holding on to the back of a chair – balance and skill come only with practice. Remember to spend more time on your weaker leg.

Next stand sideways-on and perform a low side kick with your right leg, draw it back, and kick again to the opponent's mid-section or head.

Combination techniques

Combination techniques join together the basic punches, kicks and strikes, so one technique becomes several, all aimed at different targets. When correctly performed, effective combination techniques can literally swamp the opponent's defence screen.

We are going to begin with hands-only techniques, the first being snap punch/reverse punch.

Snap punch/reverse punch

Begin from left fighting stance and:

- straighten your right knee and allow your left foot to skim forward a half-pace;

- move your right hand forward slightly;

- snap punch with your left fist even as the slide comes to a stop;

- use the slight pull back of your right fist to add power to the punch;

- twist your right hip forward and allow your left foot to slide diagonally back and out;

- strongly pull back your left fist and reverse punch with the right;

- withdraw the spent punch and reinstate your left leading guard hand.

The slide forward covers distance and the snap punch closes off the opponent's vision as it grows larger in his sight. The reverse punch is aimed at his mid-section, so he must quickly switch his attention from high to low.

Trouble Shooting

Problems	Resolutions
The snap punch is weak.	You have concentrated on the reverse punch at the expense of the snap punch. Give both techniques equal weight.
The snap punch is not sharp.	You have not used the pull-back of the lead guard hand to best effect.
The reverse punch is weak.	You did not pull back your spent punch forcefully enough and neither did you drive your right hip far enough forward.
Both punches are weak.	You have concentrated too much on performing two punches quickly. Do each single punch correctly, then aim for speed.

Step forward snap punch/reverse punch

This version of the above combination covers more distance during your advance. Begin from left fighting stance and:

- step into right fighting stance, holding your guard hands stationary as you move;

- pull back your left leading guard hand and use this to power a snap punch to the opponent's face;

- then perform a reverse punch to the opponent's mid-section.

Snap punch/snap punch

This is a clever little fist combination that uses the first punch to disguise your step forward. Begin from left fighting stance and:

- snap punch with your left fist into the opponent's face;

- synchronise the pull-back of the spent punch with a fast step forward on the right leg;

- snap punch with the right fist.

In order for this to work, your step forward must be very quick, so as to take advantage of the blind spot created by the opening punch.

Reverse punch/reverse punch

This combination is related to the one we just practised, so aim for the same combination of punch and step. Begin from a left fighting stance, then:

- reverse punch to the opponent's face with your right fist;

- use the hip twist of the punch to bring your right foot forwards even as the punch is completing (Figure 58);

Figure 58   Use the hip twist involved in the punching action to help draw your rear foot forwards.

- reverse punch to the opponent's mid-section with your left fist even as you settle into right fighting stance.

Here you must punch whilst actually on the move.

Reverse punch/back fist/reverse punch

This is a yet more complicated sequence. Begin from left fighting stance and:

- thrust forward with your right foot and skim forward a half-pace with the left;

- reverse punch to the opponent's mid-section with your right fist;

- bring your left fist to your right shoulder (Figure 59);

Figure 59   Bring your left fist to your right shoulder.

Figure 60   Slide up your trailing foot as the back fist hits the target.

- pull back the spent reverse punch and back fist to the opponent's face with your left;
- drag up your right leg as you strike the target (Figure 60);
- then step forward with your left foot and reverse punch to the opponent's mid-section with your right fist.

This combination not only confuses the opponent by aiming at high and low targets, but it also combines straight punches with turning strikes.

71

THURSDAY

Front kick/roundhouse kick

This is the simplest of the kick/kick series of combinations. Begin from a left fighting stance and:

- perform front kick with your right leg;
- withdraw the spent kick, then set it down in front of you;
- pivot on your right foot and perform a left roundhouse kick;
- withdraw the spent kick and set it down in front of you.

Each technique must be correctly performed in its own right. This means not hurrying through the sequence until you have acquired the necessary skill.

Trouble Shooting

Problems
You fall forward after each kick.

Resolutions
Keep control over your centre of gravity by keeping your support knee slightly bent, and withdraw each spent kick before you set it down.

Your technique is poor.

Slow down the combination until you can perform each kick correctly. Then begin to increase speed.

Front kick/side kick

This is slightly more difficult than the last combination because the hip has to engage more fully between the two kicks. Begin from a left fighting stance. Then:

- front kick with the right foot;
- withdraw the spent foot and set it down;
- pivot strongly with the right foot and side kick with the left foot;
- withdraw the spent foot and set it down.

Repeat this combination several times, always taking care to keep your guard under control. Concentrate on perfecting the technique before you increase the speed.

Figure 61   Set your spent kicking foot down with the hips turned away from the opponent.

Roundhouse kick/ back kick

This combination is not as difficult as it might seem because the roundhouse kick sets up the hips for the following back kick. Begin from left fighting stance and:

- perform a roundhouse kick with the right leg;

- only partly withdraw the spent kick and set it down with the hips half turned (Figure 61);

- back kick with your left foot;

- partly withdraw the spent kick and set it down;

- turn out of the kick and take up left fighting stance.

Pre-arranged sparring

Pre-arranged sparring involves one person attacking whilst another defends and counter attacks. Both parties agree beforehand who will attack, and what techniques will be used.

There are various forms of pre-arranged sparring, of which three steps is perhaps the most common. It is called 'three step' because the opponent makes three identical attacks in the form one-pause-two-pause-three. The defender makes three identical replies to the attacks but on the third, he adds a pre-arranged counter-attack.

73

THURSDAY

Three step pre-arranged sparring using inner forearm block

The opponent draws back the right leg and performs lower parry with the left arm. You remain in ready stance. Now follow the sequence:

- the opponent advances into right forward stance and attempts to punch you in the chest;
- step back with your left foot and block the punch with right inner forearm block;
- the opponent then steps forward into left forward stance and attempts a second punch;
- step back with your right foot and block with left inner forearm block;
- the opponent advances and punches for the third and last time. You step back and block with right inner forearm block;
- seize the opponent's forearm with your right hand;
- step up with your left foot and front kick the opponent's ribs using your right foot (Figure 62);

Figure 62   Slide forward with your left foot to get range, then front kick the opponent.

- drop your foot forward and perform left reverse punch to the opponent's ribs (Figure 63).

Figure 63   Reverse punch to the opponent's ribs.

Re-read the trouble shooting section on the inner block to clear up any problems.

Three step pre-arranged sparring using outer forearm block

Now try the same sequence using outer forearm block. Begin as for the previous sequence. Then:

- the opponent advances into right forward stance and attempts to punch you in the chest;
- step back with your left foot and block the punch with right outer forearm block;
- the opponent then steps forward into left forward stance and attempts a second punch;

Figure 64   Slide forward on your right foot and strike the opponent's chest with your elbow.

- step back with your right foot and block with left outer forearm block;

- the opponent advances and punches for the third and last time. You step back and block with right outer forearm block;

- twist your hips until they are at 90° to the opponent and allow your feet to slide into a straddle stance;

- bring your right arm palm downwards across your chest and extend the left palm upwards beneath it;

- then perform an elbow strike (pages 63–64) into the opponent's ribs (Figure 64).

Pre-arranged sparring using scooping block

The opponent begins from left forward stance/lower parry, then:

- the opponent performs front kick with the right foot;

- step back into right fighting stance to avoid the kick;

- the opponent performs a second front kick with the left foot and you step back into left fighting stance;

- the opponent then performs the third front kick and you step outwards with your left foot, twisting your hips and scooping the kick with your left hand;
- twist your hips back and reverse punch the opponent with your right fist.

Pre-arranged sparring using reverse parry

This sequence is very similar to the one which we have just done except in one important point – you must step back from ready stance with your right leg, and not your left. Get this wrong and the sequence won't work!

So follow the sequence:

- the opponent performs front kick with the right foot;
- step back into left fighting stance to avoid the kick;
- the opponent performs the second front kick with the left foot and you step back into right fighting stance;
- the opponent then performs the third front kick and you step diagonally outwards and backwards with your left foot;
- turn your hips in an anticlockwise direction away from the kick and draw your right foot to you, so both knees come together;
- perform lower parry with your right arm (Figure 65);
- twist your hips back, slide your right foot out and reverse punch the opponent with your left fist.

Figure 65   Draw up your right foot and perform reverse parry.

Trouble Shooting

Problems	Resolutions
The opponent's final kick caught you in the ribs.	You failed to step far enough on the diagonal and/or you were too slow.
The opponent's spent kick landed on your right knee.	You didn't draw up your right foot.
The opponent is out of range of your reverse punch.	You stepped too far back on the diagonal.

FRIDAY

LEARNING MORE ADVANCED TECHNIQUES

Two new strikes to learn

One knuckle fist

Figure 66   Extrude the middle knuckle of your middle finger and lock it out with the others.

One knuckle fist is a way of channelling all the force of a blow through a single knuckle. This makes it extremely effective against the opponent's ribs, solar plexus or temple. Make one knuckle fist by:

* rolling your fingers into a normal but loose fist;

* pushing out the middle joint of the middle finger;

* closing your fingers in on the middle finger and locking it out with your thumb (Figure 66).

Use one knuckle fist in the following way:

* the opponent steps back into left forward stance/lower parry and you remain in ready stance;

* the opponent steps forward and attempts to lunge punch you in the chest with his right fist;

- step back a short distance with your left foot, so both heels are in line and you are turned 90° to the opponent's advance;

- deflect the opponent's punch with your left forearm and at the same time, attack the opponent's solar plexus with one knuckle fist (Figure 67).

Power for the combined deflection/punch comes from the strong hip twist.

Figure 67   Use one knuckle punch to attack vulnerable points such as the solar plexus.

Palm heel

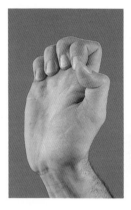

Figure 68   Curl your fingers down and draw your hand back. Fold the thumb in.

Figure 69   Use palm heel as a straight thrust to the opponent's jaw.

Palm heel can be used to attack the opponent's jaw. To form the weapon:

- bend your wrist back;

- curl your fingers and thumb into the top edge of the palm (Figure 68).

Practise palm heel from a close-up position by standing in ready stance. The opponent also stands in ready stance and takes hold of your shoulders. Then:

- grasp the opponent's left upper arm with your left;

- step back half a pace with your left foot, so your hips turn 45° to the opponent;

- strike the opponent under the jaw with palm heel (Figure 69).

Power for the palm heel comes from a combination of the step back and the hip twist.

Kicking techniques

Reverse roundhouse kick

As its name implies, reverse roundhouse kick travels along the opposite circular path to the ordinary roundhouse kick. Begin from left fighting stance and:

- draw your left foot back and in;
- transfer body weight onto the left foot;
- twist your head around to look at the target (Figure 70);

Figure 70   Twist your head around to look at the target.

Figure 71 Extend your toes and strike the side of the opponent's jaw with the sole of your foot.

- pick your right foot up and swing it along a rising circular path into the target;
- extend your toes and strike the target with the sole of your foot (Figure 71);
- continue turning your hips, flex the knee joint and withdraw the spent kick before setting it down.

83

FRIDAY

Reverse roundhouse kick is powered by a strong twisting motion of the hips – they turn through a full 180°. Adjust the range of the technique by extending or flexing your knee.

Trouble Shooting

Problems	Resolutions
The kick goes off centre.	You did not turn your hips fully into the kick.
You lose balance during the kick.	You did not transfer weight fully onto your left leg and you did not lean back far enough to counterbalance the weight of your kicking leg.
You lose balance when retrieving the spent kick.	You did not flex your knee before withdrawing it.

Foot sweep

Foot sweep is an unbalancing technique that works by jarring the opponent's foot. Both you and your partner take up left fighting stances. Then:

- deliver a fast back fist with your leading guard hand;

- follow with a reverse punch using your right fist;

- skim your right foot around in a shallow arc that strikes the opponent's Achilles' tendon and knocks his foot forward (Figure 72);

- step out with the right foot and perform left reverse punch to the back of the sprawling opponent's head.

The first reverse punch throws weight forward and releases the right foot, so it is free to move. Also, the hip action involved in reverse punch is the same as that used for the foot sweep – just allow the hips to continue circling. Strike the opponent's Achilles' tendon with the sole of your foot, curling the big toe up and depressing the others to get the correct shape.

Figure 72   Swing your right foot around and into the opponent's Achilles tendon. Guard your face!

Trouble Shooting

Problems
You strike the side of the opponent's ankle, causing him pain but not jarring him off balance.

You twist your ankle as you tried to sweep the opponent's foot.

The opponent smacks you in the face as you sweep him.

Resolutions
You didn't twist your hips enough. Your sweeping foot must curl around the back of his, knocking it forward in the direction in which it is pointing.

You did not form the correct foot shape. Strike with the sole of your foot.

Do not lean the top of your body forwards as you engage your hips.

FRIDAY

Combination techniques

Front kick/snap punch

This is surely the simplest of all the hand/foot combinations. Take up left fighting stance and:

- perform front kick with your right foot (but do not change your guard position);
- partially retrieve the kick and land forwards;
- perform snap punch even as weight descends on the new lead foot.

If you change guard as you front kick, then there will be less of a pulley action to power the snap punch.

Front kick/reverse punch

Just to confuse you, this combination **does** require you to change over your guard as you kick! Begin from left fighting stance and:

- perform front kick, and **do** change your guard hands over;
- draw back your leading hand and reverse punch with the left fist even as you land.

Reverse punch/roundhouse kick

Here, your opening punch drives the opponent back and into range of a following roundhouse kick. Begin from left fighting stance and:

- twist your hips and reach for the opponent's face with a reverse punch;
- lift your right foot and bring it around into a roundhouse kick to the side of the opponent's jaw.

The reverse punch throws your weight forward and the action required sets the hips up just right for the roundhouse kick. Aim to make the kick follow on quickly after the punch.

Side kick/back kick/reverse punch

Begin from left fighting stance and:

- pick up your right foot and bring it forward;
- twist your hips away and perform a side kick;
- partly withdraw the side kick and set it down in a lead position, but keep your hips turned;

- twist your hips and perform a back kick with your left foot;
- set the spent kicking foot down and twist strongly about-face;
- use the twisting action to drive out a strong reverse punch.

Side kick engages the hips and provided you do not fully retrieve the spent kick, they will also be set up for the following back kick. Remember to transfer weight forwards as you perform the final reverse punch.

Roundhouse kick/back kick/back fist/reverse punch

Begin from left fighting stance and launch a long reaching roundhouse kick to the opponent's head with your right foot. Then:

- keep your hips twisted as you drop the spent kick to the floor in lead position;
- twist strongly around and back kick with your left foot;
- drop the foot diagonally behind your right and twist about-face;
- use the twisting action to power a back fist with the left hand;
- complete the combination with a powerful reverse punch.

This is quite a difficult combination insofar as it combines linear with circular techniques. The most common error is to fail to focus the back fist to a sharp stop.

Pre-arranged sparring

Though the following can be done in a three-step sequence, you might care to try them in the form of a single step block and counter-attack.

Head block against lunge punch – 1

The opponent steps back into left forward stance and performs a left lower parry. You remain in ready stance. Then the opponent steps forward with the right foot and attempts a lunge punch into your face:

- step diagonally back and out with your right foot and take up a straddle stance;
- punch upwards with your left fist, so you take the punch on your forearm;
- continue the deflection so it becomes a punch into the opponent's jaw (Figure 73);

FRIDAY

Figure 73   Use the blocking arm to perform a curving punch.

Figure 74   Pull her head down and knee her in the face.

- twist your hips until they both face her directly;
- reach forward with both hands and take her shoulders;
- pull her head down and knee her in the face with your right leg (Figure 74).

This is an advanced sequence in that the block and part of the counter-attack are simultaneous. This theme also recurs in the second example.

FRIDAY

Head block against lunge punch – 2

Begin as for the previous example. Then as the opponent punches to your face:

- step back and around with your right foot;

- use your left hand to punch over the top of the opponent's punch, so you deflect her attack and score with your own (Figure 75);

- withdraw your left fist, draw back your left foot to a position of balance and use your right foot for a roundhouse kick (Figure 76).

Figure 75   Punch over the top of the opponent's attack.

Figure 76   Draw back your left foot and perform roundhouse kick with the right.

FRIDAY

Scooping block against one-step front kick

The opponent begins by stepping back into left fighting stance. Then she performs one-step front kick to your mid-section. Respond by:

- taking a long diagonal step backwards and to the left with your left foot even as she is stepping (Figure 77);

Figure 77   Take a long diagonal step back with your left foot. Maintain your guard!

- then as she kicks twist right around with your hips and scoop her kick with your right hand;
- twist right back around and use your left fist in a reverse punch counter-attack.

Stand well back from the opponent because a one-step kick covers a lot of ground. Also take a large step backwards, or you will be in the wrong position to block her.

Reverse parry against one-step front kick

Begin as for the previous technique and as the opponent takes her step towards you:

- take a large diagonal step backwards and out to the right with your right foot (Figure 78);

- as she kicks, turn your hips away clockwise and draw up your left foot;

- deflect the opponent's kick with your left arm;

- slide your left leg back towards the opponent, twist your hips and strike her with a right-hand reverse punch.

Figure 78   Step back and out with the rear foot as the opponent steps forward.

PREPARING TO FREE SPAR

Two further strikes to learn

Knife hand

We have already come across knife hand in the form of a block but this time, we will look at how it can be used as a strike. The opponent takes up left forward stance/lower parry and advances into you with lunge punch to the head. Take up ready stance and even as he moves:

- step back smartly with your right foot;

- bend your left elbow and bring it palm downwards across the front of your chest;

- bring your right hand back to your right ear, as though saluting (Figure 79);

Figure 79   Bring your right hand back to your ear.

Figure 80   Use hip action to help power knife hand to the opponent's neck.

- twist your hips strongly and deflect the opponent's punch with the side of your left wrist whilst simultaneously striking to the side of the opponent's neck (Figure 80).

In keeping with the more advanced sequences which we are now looking at, this combines the block with the counter-attack. The trick is to delay the twisting of your hips until your right foot has been correctly placed.

93

SATURDAY

You can use knife strike in a slightly different way if you are facing the wrong way. Imagine that you have just delivered right lunge punch to one opponent, but that another opponent is behind you:

- step back with your leading right foot, so it brushes past the left;
- continue on stepping back and take up a straddle stance;
- fold your right arm across your chest and turn your hand palm upwards so the fingers are near the side of your jaw. Let your left arm move across your stomach (Figure 81);

Figure 81   Fold your right arm across your front.

*Figure 82   Turn your hips towards the opponent whilst drawing
back your left hand and striking with the right.*

- pull your left fist back to the hip and use this action to help power a
  horizontal knife strike to the side of the opponent's throat (Figure 82).

This version twists the hand palm downwards on impact, whereas the
previous strike turned the hand palm upwards. Power for this latter
strike comes from a combination of hip twist with pull-back of the non-
striking arm.

Spear hand

Spear hand uses the same hand shape as knife hand. This time, however,
impact is made on the tips of the fingers. But spread the force over three
fingers by slightly drawing back the middle one.

Deliver spear hand with the thumb upwards, with the palm downwards,
or with the palm upwards, and use it to attack vulnerable targets such as
the floating ribs, the groin and the solar plexus. Try the following:

- take up straddle stance;

- extend your left arm and hand to your left side until the fingers are at
  the height of the opponent's groin;

95

*Figure 83   Step across
the front of your left leg
with your right but don't
move your arms.*

- turn your left hand palm downwards and carry the right palm upwards on your chest;
- step across the front of your left leg with the right, but don't move your arms (Figure 83);
- continue through into right straddle stance so that you are facing in the other direction;
- just before you settle into the new stance, pull back your left hand and rotate it palm upwards;
- at exactly the same time and speed, thrust out your right hand and rotate it palm downwards.

Gain further practice by stepping from stance to stance.

SATURDAY

Kicking techniques

Step up reverse roundhouse kick

Take up left fighting stance and:

- snap punch with your left fist into the opponent's face;

- even as you are punching, bring your right foot forwards so the heels touch (Figure 84);

- lift your left foot up and swing it around in a curving kick to the side of the opponent's face.

The snap punch functions as a feint, hiding the step up that brings you into kicking range.

Figure 84 Use the snap punch to disguise the slide-up of your rear foot.

Reverse foot sweep

Both parties take up left fighting stance. Then:

- reverse punch to the opponent's face with your right fist;
- skim your right foot around and attempt to sweep the opponent's leading left leg;
- the opponent sees your sweep and lifts her foot, so your foot passes under it (Figure 85);
- drop the spent sweep to the floor and spin around on it, so your back turns to the opponent;

Figure 85   The opponent sees your foot sweep and lifts her foot.

Figure 86   Continue turning and sweep her supporting leg.

- sweep her supporting leg with your left leg (Figure 86).

This is a spectacular technique that tumbles the opponent onto her back. It works because she is standing on one leg as your left thigh slams into her.

Pre-arranged sparring

Pre-arranged sparring is now becoming quite realistic. Neither punches nor kicks are obligingly left extended for you to operate upon. Each technique is performed at full speed from fighting stance and pulled back, so correct timing and distance are essential.

SATURDAY

Checking kick against snap punch

Face the opponent in fighting stance. There is no need for either of you to lead with any particular foot. The opponent inches towards you and then settles. Then:

- the opponent sprints forward and attempts to snap punch you in the face;
- you transfer all your body weight over the back leg and draw your lead foot in (Figure 87);

Figure 87   Rock back onto your rear foot and draw in the leading foot.

- front kick with your leading foot into the opponent's solar plexus.

It helps if you take up quite a long opening stance, so the pull-back of body weight takes you out of range of the punch.

Do not attempt to block the punch! In a real life situation, fast punches are almost impossible to block.

SATURDAY

Roundhouse kick against reverse punch

Normally one would never kick when the opponent is in punching range, but this sequence shows how to open distance and counter attack. Both parties take up left fighting stance and the opponent attempts to close into reverse punch range. Then:

- the opponent throws his weight forward and attempts to reverse punch you in the mid-section with his right fist;
- quickly draw back your left foot until both heels touch;
- then use your right foot to perform roundhouse kick to the opponent's head.

It helps if you take up a long fighting stance because when you withdraw, you will take yourself out of range of the punch.

Reverse parry defence against front kick

Both partners take up left stance. Then the opponent aims a powerful front kick at your mid-section. Respond by:

- thrusting forward with your right foot to the outside of your opponent;
- allowing your left foot to skim diagonally forwards and out;
- blocking down with your right arm to deflect the kick (Figure 88);

Figure 88   Step diagonally forward and out, and block with your right arm.

- twisting your hips around in a clockwise direction and reverse punching the opponent.

The opponent began in left fighting stance, kicked with her right foot and so completes in right stance. Her right side is now said to be her 'closed side' because there are no foot or fist weapons that she can quickly use to defend herself. Whenever possible, always move to the opponent's closed side.

Barring block against front kick

Both parties take up left fighting stance. Then:

- the opponent launches a full-speed front kick aimed at your mid-section;

- even as you see the foot rising, thrust forward with your right leg and allow the left to skim forwards a half pace;

- catch the opponent's kicking knee with your left forearm, so it is prevented from rising to kicking height;

- simultaneously strike the opponent's solar plexus with a one knuckle punch (Figure 89).

This technique will only work if you crowd the opponent, so she is forced to kick from a shorter distance than she might otherwise have preferred. Failure to close with her will mean that her shin catches you in the groin!

Figure 89   Bar down on the opponent's rising knee and punch over the top.

Thrusting block against roundhouse kick

Like the previous sequence, this uses a hand technique to prevent the development of the opponent's attack. Both partners begin from left fighting stance. Then:

- the opponent attempts to perform roundhouse kick to your head with her right foot;

- thrust forward with your right foot and allow your left to skim forward;

- strike the opponent in the centre of her chest with the edge of your left hand (Figure 90).

The opponent must turn across you as she kicks and if you time things right, you will strike her in the centre of her chest with your counter.

Figure 90   Advance into the opponent's kick and drive her backwards with the edge of your hand.

SUNDAY

PUTTING IT ALL TOGETHER

Sunday's session sees the culmination of the week's training expressed through free sparring. Successful free sparring can only result when you:

- have mastered the basic techniques;
- can put them together into logical combinations;
- have practised pre-arranged sparring and understood the concepts of distance and timing.

The equipment you will need

Safe sparring means wearing a certain amount of defensive padding to protect vulnerable areas. Everyone should buy a pair of fist mitts but only choose those with no more than one centimetre of padding. The thumb must not be covered by padding.

Soft, flexible shin guards may also be worn. You can buy shin pads that extend down to cover the instep and these are useful for protecting your foot, though they may make front kick more difficult to perform.

Male students should wear a boxer type of groin guard – but not the plastic cups which slip into a jock. Women are advised to buy a plastic breast shield, or to wear a padded jacket. Properly fitted gumshields are also advisable, especially when you are fighting people from outside of your home club.

Sparring and safety

No one may wear spectacles whilst sparring – even when these have plastic lenses. Soft contact lenses are allowed on the wearer's own responsibility (but beware – they almost always become dislodged!). Earrings, necklaces, bracelets or any other jewellery must be removed. Any ring that will not come off must be taped over.

Long hair must be secured with an elastic band and all hair grips and hard fasteners should be removed. Finger- and toenails must be both short and clean.

No one is allowed to chew during sparring because of the risk of choking.

No sparring should take place on a bare stone or concrete floor surface.

SUNDAY

The protocols of free sparring

Free sparring is not a free-for-all! It is a co-operative exercise in which two exponents try to sharpen their skills against each other. In order to prevent it from degenerating into a brawl, a number of simple rules are put into action. These can be summarised as follows:

- the force of all techniques is to be controlled. This is especially important where face punches and head kicks are used. Such techniques are allowed only the lightest touch;

- open-handed attacks to the face are not allowed;

- attacks to the opponent's limbs and joints are not allowed;

- attacks to the throat and groin are not allowed;

- head butts are prohibited;

- you may not seize and hold on to the opponent;

- all clean and controlled hits on the opponent's face and body must be acknowledged by a momentary disengagement and a brief nod;

- continuous back pedalling is not allowed;

- neither person is allowed to step outside of the area, except when propelled out;

- both parties must take proper care for their own safety. This means maintaining an effective guard at all times;

- senior grades must not physically abuse lower grades, and neither must lower grades take advantage of high grades who are exercising restraint;

- where there is a large difference in size, then both participants must take extra care for their own safety;

- malice or lack of respect have no place in the karate training hall.

By means of these rules, free sparring becomes an enjoyable part of training.

Tactics to use

Distance

Fight at a distance which suits you, and/or which is unsuitable for the opponent. For instance this means crowding taller opponents, so their longer reach is of no advantage to them. Keep well back from those who favour punches, so they are forced always to step forward, or to rely on kicks.

SUNDAY

Don't let the opponent corner you. Always move as far as is necessary to make an attack miss – but no further!

Timing

The aggressive fighter will move in as soon as you begin a technique – but watch out for feints! Always look at the opponent's head and shoulders and when they move, be ready.

The defensive fighter waits until the opponent's technique has failed, then moves in even as it is being retrieved. Kicks take a long time to pull back and until they are, the opponent's defensive screen will be weak. But never move too far away as you avoid the attack, or it will take too long to close again.

If you are naturally an aggressive fighter, then practise to be a defensive fighter too because that way, you will double your capabilities.

Line

Always try and inch your way on to the closed side of the opponent, so he always has to turn before he can launch a technique at you. Practise this by taking up left fighting stance against someone in left stance, and by moving until both your front feet are in line. Then turn your body slightly so you face the opponent directly. He is now turned slightly away from you.

You will have to adjust your line constantly as the session continues, but avoid making your efforts noticeable.

Targeting

Straight punches into the face close off the opponent's view. Circular strikes are not nearly so effective, though they can creep in around the very edge of the opponent's defensive screen.

Aim your front kicks high and to the side of the opponent's chest, where they are difficult to block.

Combinations

Overload the opponent's defensive screen by a flurry of effective techniques. These must arrive at their targets in quick succession, otherwise the opponent will see them as single techniques and advantage will be lost. Space the attacking techniques out, so one goes for the face and the second to the low stomach, etc. This makes the opponent switch his attention from high to low. Mix circular with straight techniques to make things even more difficult for him.

Psyching out the opponent

Try stamping down hard with your lead foot, as though you intend to go in at the opponent. How does he react? If he pulls back from you, then he is a defensive fighter and you should hold back, so he has to switch onto the attack. If he advances towards you, then he is an attacking fighter and you should immediately put him on the defensive.

Vary your fighting habits

All of us have favourite techniques and tactics and these tend to appear during every sparring session. Make sure the opponent doesn't suss out your next move by being too predictable.

Future development of your karate practice

This book will give you a thorough grounding in the basic techniques, combinations and pair-form practice of karate. Even so, it cannot replace the benefits to be gained from training at a proper karate club. There you will learn the other great building block of the art – the karate **kata**. I would like to have included kata in this book, but the format would not lend itself well to the idea.

So use this book to provide yourself with an invaluable introduction to your formal practice, and that way you'll keep well ahead of the club training syllabus!

GLOSSARY

Ashi Barai *Ashy barreye* Foot sweep
Ate *Ahtay* Strike

Barai *Barreye* Sweep or parry

Chudan *Chew-dan* Stomach and chest

Do *Dough* Way
Dojo *Dough joe* Training place

Empi *Em-pee* Elbow

Gamae *Gam-my* Stance
Gedan *Gay-dan* Groin and thighs
Gi *gee* Karate suit
Gyakuzuki *Gee-akoo-ski* Reverse punch

Hanmei gamae *Han-mee gam-my* Fighting stance
Hidari *Hid-darry* Left

Ipponken *Ippon-ken* One knuckle punch

Jodan *Joe-dan* Face and head
Junzuki *Jun-ski* Lunge punch

Karate *Kah-rah-tay* Way of the empty hand
Karategi *Kah-rah-tay gee* Karate tunic
Keri *Kerry* Kick
Kibadachi *Kee-bah dachy* Straddle or horseriding stance
Kihon *Kee-hon* Punch
Kiritsu *Kirrits* Stand up
Kizamezuki *Kizamma-ski* Snap punch
Kohai *Koe-high* Junior grade
Kokutsudachi *Koksoo-dachy* Back stance
Kumite *Koo-mittay* Sparring

Maegeri *My-gerry* Front kick
Mawashigeri *Mah-wash-igerry* Roundhouse kick
Mokuso *Mock-so* Meditation
Migi *Miggy* Right

Nekoashi *Nekko-ashy* Cat stance
Nori *Naw-ree* Attention stance
Nukite *Noo-kittay* Spear hand

Oi tsuki *Oy-ski* Lunge punch
Otogai ni rei *Oh-toggeye knee ray* Bow to classmates

109

GLOSSARY

Rei   *Ray*   Bow
Renraku Waza   *Ren-rack wazza*   Combination technique

Seiza   *Say-za*   Kneel
Sempai   *Sem-pie*   Senior grade
Sensei   *Sen-say*   Teacher
Sensei ni rei   *Sen-say knee ray*   Bow to the teacher
Shuto   *Sh'toe*   Knife hand

Taisho   *Tie-sho*   Palm heel
Tettsui   *Tet soo-ee*   Hammer fist
Tsurikomi   *Soo-rih-koe-mee*   One step
Tobikomizuki   *Tobby kommy ski*   Snap punch

Uke   *'Keh*   Block
Uraken   *Oorah-ken*   Back fist
Ushirogeri   *Oosheeroe-gerry*   Back kick

Yamei   *Yammay*   Stop
Yoi   *Yoy*   Ready stance
Yokogeri   *Yoko-gerry*   Side kick

Zenkutsudachi   *Zen-kutsoo-dachy*   Forward stance
Zuki   *Z'ki*   Punch

SOME USEFUL ADDRESSES

The English Karate Governing Body
PO Box 1824
Arnos Grove
London N11 1QB
Tel: 081 882 8491.

The Martial Arts Commission
Broadway House
15–16 Deptford Broadway
London SE8 4PE
Tel: 081 691 3433.

The Northern Ireland Martial Arts Commission
House of Sport
Upper Malone Road
Belfast BT9 5LA
Tel: 0232 381222.

The Scottish Karate Board of Control
c/o The Sports Council
Caledonia House
South Gyle
Edinburgh EH12 9DW
Tel: 031 317 7200.

The Welsh Karate Federation
Smalldrink
Parsonage Lane
Begelly
Kilgetty
Dyfed
Tel: 0834 813776.